The Robotx

Get Help from Simple Machines

Rolling Along

The Wheel and Axle

Written by Gerry Bailey   Illustrated by Mike Spoor

The Robotx
Get Help from Simple Machines

Crabtree Publishing Company
www.crabtreebooks.com
1-800-387-7650

PMB 59051, 350 Fifth Ave.
59th Floor,
New York, NY 10118

616 Welland Ave.
St. Catharines, ON
L2M 5V6

Published by Crabtree Publishing in 2014

Author: Gerry Bailey
Illustrator: Mike Spoor
Editor: Kathy Middleton
Proofreader: Crystal Sikkens
End matter: Kylie Korneluk
**Production coordinator and
   Prepress technician:** Ken Wright
Print coordinator: Margaret Amy Salter

Photographs:
All images are Shutterstock.com unless otherwise stated.
Pg 18 – (l) Ingvar Bjork (r) OPIS Zagreb
Pg 19 – (tl) Thomas Barrat (tr) Alexander Kuguchin (bl) aodaodaodaod (br) HomeArt
Pg 21 – (t) Chubykin Arkady (b) Jason Benz Bennee
Pg 27 – Voronin76

Printed in Canada/022014/MA20131220

Library and Archives Canada Cataloguing in Publication

Bailey, Gerry, author
     Rolling along : the wheel and axle / written by Gerry Bailey ; illustrated by Mike Spoor.

(The robotx get help from simple machines)
Includes index.
Issued in print and electronic formats.
ISBN 978-0-7787-0418-8 (bound).--ISBN 978-0-7787-0424-9 (pbk.).--ISBN 978-1-4271-7536-6 (pdf).--ISBN 978-1-4271-7530-4 (html)

     1. Wheels--Juvenile literature. 2. Axles--Juvenile literature.
I. Spoor, Mike, illustrator II. Title.

TJ181.5.B35 2014   j621.8   C2013-908713-3
                                          C2013-908714-1

Library of Congress Cataloging-in-Publication Data

Bailey, Gerry, author.
 Rolling along : the wheel and axle / written by Gerry Bailey ; illustrated by Mike Spoor.
      pages cm. -- (The Robotx get help from simple machines)
 Audience: Ages 5-8.
 Audience: K to grade 3.
 Includes index.
 ISBN 978-0-7787-0418-8 (reinforced library binding) -- ISBN 978-0-7787-0424-9 (pbk.) -- ISBN 978-1-4271-7536-6 (electronic pdf) -- ISBN 978-1-4271-7530-4 (electronic html)
 1. Wheels--Juvenile literature. 2. Axles--Juvenile literature. 3. Simple machines--Juvenile literature. I. Spoor, Mike, illustrator. II. Title. III. Title: Wheels and axles.

 TJ181.5.B35 2014
 621.8'11--dc23
                                          2013050838

Contents

The
Robotx

Meet   and

RobbO   RobbEE

The robots' workshop

RobbO is excited. All of the parts have just been delivered to the workshop to make his new machine.

RobbO is going to build a whizz-fizz machine with help from RobbEE.

A machine is...

A machine is a tool used to make work easier. Work is the effort needed to create force. A force is a push or pull on an object. Machines allow us to push, pull, or lift a heavy weight much easier, or using less effort. All machines are made up of at least one **simple machine**.

There are six kinds of simple machines. Some have just one part that moves. Others are made up of two or more parts. The six simple machines are:

- **lever**
- **pulley**
- **inclined plane**
- **wheel and axle**
- **wedge**
- **screw**

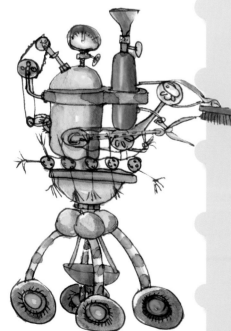

Read on to learn about the wheel and axle.

It's RobbEE's job to carry all of the parts into the workshop.

So much stuff!

Phew! It's hard work.
He gets so tired he has
to stop a lot to recharge
his battery for energy.

"Hurry," says RobbO, who can't wait to get started on his new **invention**.

RobbEE tries carrying several boxes at a time, but they're too heavy.

He tries dragging them and pushing them, but gets just as run down.

"RobbEE, you can make things a lot easier if you use the wheels," says RobbO.

"Of course!" says RobbEE (who had forgotten all about the wheels).
"I'll use wheels!"

"Here," says RobbO, who knows just what to do. "You need to use a wheel and axle. First, you connect two wheels with a rod called an axle."

"These go in the front.

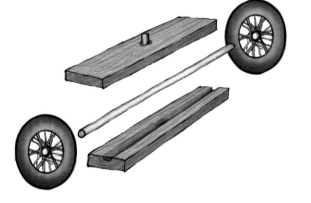

Then you connect two more wheels to another axle. These go at the back."

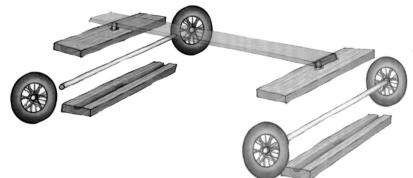

"Use wooden boards with grooves to cover the axles, then join the two axles with a longer wooden board."

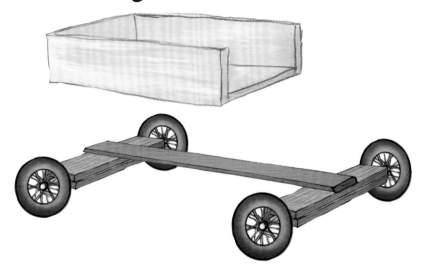

"Finally, attach a box to the top." Ta-da! RobbO has made a cart!

Now RobbEE can pile the cart high, and it's easy to pull it along.

After a few loads, the job is finished.

Wheels and friction

Friction happens when two things rub together. The amount of friction created depends on the weight of the load and the kind of surface it is moving over.

direction of motion

force of friction

Friction is a force that makes things slow down. Whatever direction an object is moving in, friction pulls in the opposite direction.

Wheels make moving a load much easier and faster. The object is lifted up, and only the wheels touch the ground. This creates less friction.

RobbO tells RobbEE they can have fun with the cart. They can use it like a **soapbox racer** to run downhill.

First, he adds a seat to the back of the cart. Then he attaches the front axle with a screw in the middle. This allows the axle to turn.

Finally, he attaches a cord to each end of the axle.

Now RobbO can steer his cart. To turn right, he pulls on the right-hand cord. To turn left, he pulls on the left-hand cord.

It's lots of fun riding downhill together.

The spinning wheel

The Robotx take a break. RobbO tells his friend a story about a spinning wheel.

Long ago there lived a beautiful young woman named Arachne. Not only was she beautiful, she was an expert at spinning **thread** and **weaving** cloth. Arachne liked to brag about her skill. She even claimed she could spin and weave better than the goddess Athena!

This made Athena angry. Disguised as an old woman the goddess visited Arachne and told her to be careful about bragging that she could compete with a goddess.

16

This made Arachne angry, too. She said she would challenge Athena any day. With that, the goddess threw off her disguise and accepted Arachne's challenge.

Athena had to admit that Arachne was good, but she wanted to punish her for being too proud.

So the goddess told Arachne that because she loved to spin and weave, Athena would make her spin forever. Then the goddess turned the shocked girl into a spider.

And since that time, all spiders have had to live in the webs they spin.

Wheels and axles

A wheel and axle can be used to move an object from place to place, to drive a machine, or to create power.

The waterwheel is an ancient device that uses a wheel and axle. Blades or buckets are attached all the way around a huge wheel. As it turns, water is lifted out of the river.

A rolling pin is a cylinder-shaped wheel on an axle with handles at each end. The long cylinder spreads the effort over a larger area.

Windmills use a circle of blades on an axle to catch wind. They make power or pump water.

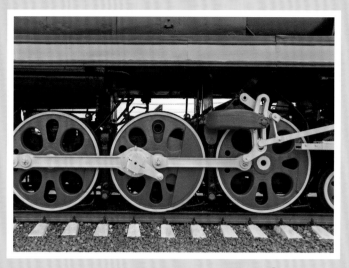

On steam trains, the force created by the steam moves a rod which moves a series of wheel and axles.

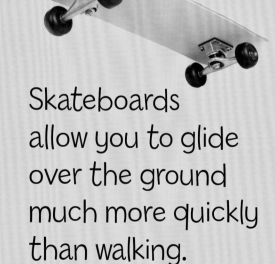

An axle controls the flow of water when a tap is turned.

Skateboards allow you to glide over the ground much more quickly than walking.

Fun-time wheels

RobbO knows where there is a large wheel and axle they can have fun with. It's the roundabout in the park. A roundabout is a wheel that lies on its side. It spins on an axle that's attached in an upright position.

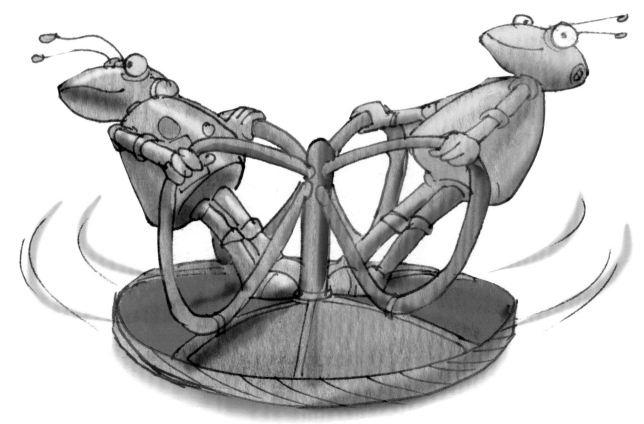

A Ferris wheel is a huge wheel with seats around its edge. It turns very slowly on an axle. People sit in the seats for an exciting ride.

A merry-go-round, or carousel, is a wheel that spins on an axle in an upright position.

In the toolbox

These tools don't look like wheels, but they all use wheel and axle movements to do their work.

Screwdriver

The handle of a screwdriver acts as the wheel. When you turn it, the wheel turns the shaft, or long arm. The shaft is the axle.

Hand drill

A hand drill has a bent handle that turns in a large circle like a wheel. The axle is the drill bit, or cutting piece, which is turned in a smaller circle.

Doorknob

A round doorknob is a wheel. An axle, or rod, connects one knob to another knob on the other side of the door. When you turn a knob, the axle turns and moves the latch inside that holds a door shut.

Wrench

A wrench doesn't look like a wheel and axle until it is attached to a bolt. The bolt becomes the axle. When you turn the wrench, it acts as the wheel and turns the bolt to tighten its hold.

Robbo's science workshop

The robots and all their friends have gathered at the workshop to learn about the wheel and axle.

The wheel and axle is a simple machine that helps you turn things. The axle goes through the center of the wheel. When one of these parts is turned, the other part turns, too.

This is how it works. The radius of the wheel—that's the measurement from the center of the wheel to its edge—is longer than the radius of the axle.

When you turn a doorknob (the wheel), the knob's larger turning movement creates a smaller, but more powerful, turning movement of the rod (the axle). This makes a door easier to open.

24

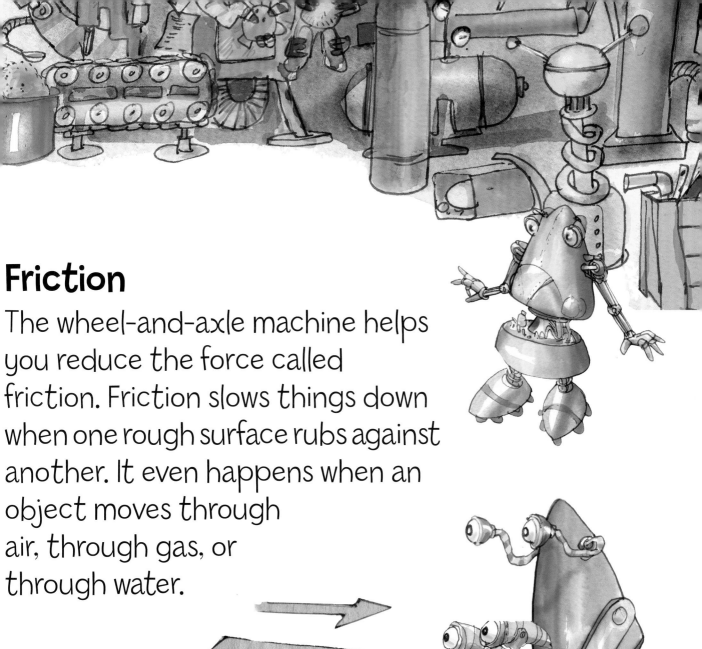

Friction

The wheel-and-axle machine helps you reduce the force called friction. Friction slows things down when one rough surface rubs against another. It even happens when an object moves through air, through gas, or through water.

Friction makes objects heat up, too.

Wheels turning wheels

Sometimes wheels have teeth cut around their edges. These wheels are called cogs, sprockets, or gears.

The teeth of each gear fit into one another, and the turning movement is passed on from gear to gear.

turns clockwise

Gears are also used to change the direction of wheels, as well as the speed at which they move.

turns counterclockwise

Inside a **mechanical** clock, there are gears that turn the hands to show the time of day.

Two simple machines working together

A bicycle uses two kinds of simple machines. It has several sets of wheel and axles, as well as another kind of simple machine called a lever.

Two of the wheel and axle sets are the big wheels at the front and back that have tires.

gear

Another wheel and axle set is the gear attached to the back wheel. A chain loops around this gear as well as the gear at the pedals. When you push on the pedals, it moves the chain and turns the back wheel.

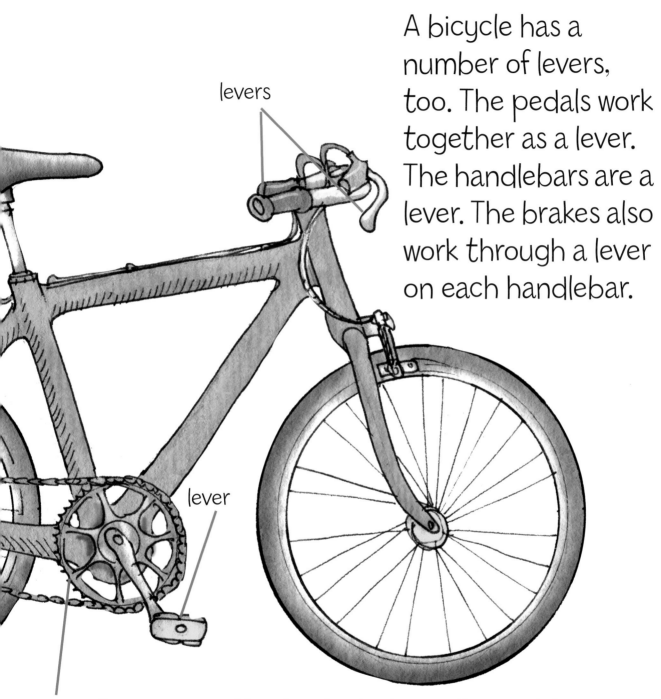

levers

A bicycle has a number of levers, too. The pedals work together as a lever. The handlebars are a lever. The brakes also work through a lever on each handlebar.

lever

gear

Squeezing the brake lever pulls a cable attached to brake blocks. These grip the sides of the wheel slowing it down using friction.

29

Build a super-cycle

RobbO has a plan. He puts all the wheel and axle ideas together and builds a super-cycle time machine. It's his most useful invention yet!

RobbO turns the pedals. The pedals turn the gears, which turn the chains, which turn the hands of the clock.

Learning more

Books

Wheels and Axles
By Kay Manolis
(Scholastic, 2010)

How Toys Work: Wheels and Axles
By Sian Smith
(Heinemann, 2012)

Wheels and Axles
By Daisy Allyn
(Gareth Stevens Publishing, 2013)

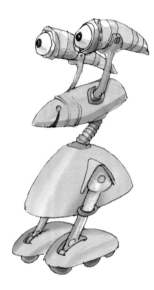

Websites

www.brainpop.com/technology/simplemachines
Activities that provide examples of wheels and axles
and what they do.

teacher.scholastic.com/dirtrep/Simple/wheel.htm
Information on wheels and axles and how they are used.

www.mocomi.com/wheel-an-axle/
A short animated clip and description on wheels
and axles.

Glossary

inclined plane A slanted surface connecting a lower point to a higher point

invention Something that has been created

lever A bar that rests on a support called a fulcrum which lifts or moves loads

mechanical Something operated by a machine

pulley A simple machine that uses grooved wheels and a rope to raise, lower, or move a load

screw An inclined plane wrapped around a pole which holds things together or lifts materials

simple machine A machine that makes work easier by transferring force from one point to another

soapbox racer A motorless car that uses gravity as the force to move it forward

thread A fine strand of material

weaving To form by interlacing threads, yarns, strands, or strips of material

wedge Two inclined planes joined together used to split things

wheel and axle A wheel with a rod, called an axle, through its center which lifts or moves loads

Index